Find Us On Pinterest

Find Us On Pinterest

ALSO BY SPENCER COFFMAN

A Guide To Deception
Relax And Unwind
Work Less Live More
A Healthier You!
Affiliate Marketing Expert
More Facebook Everything
365 Days Of Devotion For Everyone
YouTube Takeover

Find Us On Pinterest

FIND US ON PINTEREST

5 Steps To Creating
An Effective Pinterest Presence

BY
SPENCER COFFMAN

While every precaution has been taken in the preparation of this book, the author and/or publisher assumes no responsibility for errors or omissions, or for damages resulting from the use of the information contained herein.

FIND US ON PINTEREST: 5 STEPS TO CREATING AN EFFECTIVE PINTEREST PRESENCE

First edition. February 2018.

ISBN: 978-1-9814918-5-8 (Paperback)
ISBN: 978-1-3866688-1-7 (Digital)

Written by Spencer Coffman.
SpencerCoffman.com

Would you like to position your business for a whole new level of success?

How about dominating the most effective Pinterest marketing techniques?

This step-by-step Pinterest training system is going to take you by the hand and show you how to skyrocket your online presence in the shortest time ever!

- Do you want to get the most out of Pinterest and don't know when or how do it?

- Are you struggling to find a proven and trusted training system about Pinterest?

- Do you have a hard time knowing what to do with your current Pinterest followers?

Read on as I reveal how you can quickly and effectively build your Pinterest foundation to improve your business.

Nowadays, the success of your business depends on the quality of traffic to your website, in addition to social recognition your business receives.

You could have the best business, product, or service.

However...

If you don't have a good social media presence you're missing out!

Pinterest was made to help businesses succeed in marketing to it millions of users. It is a social media platform that advertises based on word of mouth – The best form of advertising!

90% of consumers trust recommendations while only 14% trust advertisements!

Erik Qualman, author of Socialnomics, has stated that socialnomics means, "Word of mouth on digital steroids."

Considering that people trust recommendations more than advertisements you need to make sure that what is being shared on social media is what you want others to share.

In reality, you don't have a choice whether or not your business is on social media. The question is how well your business appears on social media.

If your presence is poor, you could be doing some serious harm to your business.

Therefore, you need to take control of your Pinterest presence and this great book will help you do exactly that!

Introducing:

Find Us On Pinterest

You'll discover...

- Really hot facts about Pinterest that will blow you away.

- What exactly do you do on Pinterest?

- The exact questions you should be able to answer to market to your customers.

- What type of account should you create on Pinterest?

- How to optimize your profile, boards, and pins.

- How to use Pinterest to appear in search engine results.

- The best ways to get lots of followers.

- And so much more!!!

Stop worrying about whether or not you are properly set up on Pinterest. Use this book as your guide to building the best Pinterest account possible.

Now you can control what goes on social media and you will be able to take advantage of the word of mouth marketing that occurs on Pinterest.

So if you want to...

- Quickly and safely grow a huge army of potential clients or customers 100% targeted to your business.

- Productively interact with your new and existing clients or customers in order to scale your business to a whole new level of success.

- Use Pinterest as an extension of your website to help boost your SEO, rank, and online presence.

Then this book is for you!

There are five very easy to follow steps that will take you from starting a brand new Pinterest account to promoting that account to get lots of highly targeted followers.

This is a great chance for you to discover the best and most effective techniques you can use on Pinterest.

Claim Your Copy Today

But First...

How much do you think it would cost to make your business known to thousands of people?

How much do you think you'll spend on Pinterest to get all of these followers?

ABSOLUTELY NOTHING

That's right you can do it 100% free.

All you need is this book. It will show you everything you need to know. Save yourself countless amounts of time and hours of frustration. Learn from someone else. It's as simple as that.

"Yes! I really want to start creating an amazing Pinterest account so that I can use it to boost my online presence and SEO rankings.

So please send me my copy of "Find Us On Pinterest" - so I can get started building my account and increase my followers right away!

Claim Your Copy Today!

Find Us On Pinterest

Find Us On Pinterest

Table of Contents

Table of Contents

Find Us On Pinterest

Introduction

Pinterest is an amazing platform that has become very popular and is growing to become even more popular. People know they can find anything they want on Pinterest and every day millions of people search for recipes, craft ideas, products, food, travel, clothing, and a lot more. People spend hours upon hours browsing for ideas and inspiration. Other people spend hours posting content to give others ideas and inspiration. There is one thing that all of these Pinterest posts, or "pins", have in common and that is a picture.

A Pinterest pin is a picture. That is it. People love pictures and Pinterest is full of them so people love Pinterest. The saying "a picture is worth a thousand words" holds true. Of course, people can add descriptions to their pins but many people simply don't take the time. Most people share something to Pinterest and allow Pinterest to append the link and leave it be. This is fine because when people are browsing they rarely open up a pin. Usually, people can decide whether or not they like it based on the photo.

Find Us On Pinterest

Pinterest has centered their entire business model and platform around the notion that pictures are always hot. They know that no matter what, people will always spend the time to look at pictures. Whether it is a picture of a product, a funny photo, or some family memory, people will spend time looking at them, sharing them, and saving them.

The makers of Pinterest have invested millions and millions of dollars in order to build an outstanding platform. They have done lots of research and had many tests to find out exactly what users like and what works best. In fact, Pinterest is built and liked so well that many online sales platforms have copied their design. Letgo is one such place that has copied the design right down to the fact that users don't even need to add titles or descriptions!

Using Pinterest to help market your business is a great way to get people interested in whatever you have to offer. Clearly, you already understand the impact that Pinterest can have on your business or you wouldn't be dedicating the time to learn more about using it effectively. Either way, sharing your photos on Pinterest can really help your business. As long as you are sharing them well and are working to build a following, that is.

The question then becomes, how do you do that? Well, that is what this entire book is dedicated to. It will help you effectively build your Pinterest presence so you can market successfully on Pinterest. By setting up a good Pinterest base, you will be able to grow a huge force of clients that are specifically targeted to whatever it is you offer. This will create better customers and a much better business experience. After all, if you don't set up a good base then later on your tower will crumble. Therefore, use the steps in this book to build a solid foundation and use Pinterest as a pillar for your business.

The great thing about Pinterest is that we know your followers will be specifically targeted to your business. They are almost certain to become customers. This is because someone is only going to start following you if they like the content you are pinning. Therefore, the people who start following you because they like your pins obviously have an interest in your business. As long as you are posting business related pins, that is. Thus, these followers are targeted customers. Now, does that mean they will always buy from you? No, however, they will be much more likely to make a purchase than a random Pinterest user.

Pinterest is a wonderful platform that you can use to help fulfill many of your business marketing goals. They have many powerful tools created especially for businesses that you can use to gain a new level of interaction with your clients. Having a good Pinterest presence isn't going to be a walk in the park. It is going to be a walk through Central Park in the middle of the night. There will be some dark paths, rough patches, and difficulty. However, if you persevere and work through it, then you will start seeing results. That is a fact.

This book is not going to be sugar-coated. It is going to tell you exactly what you can do to help you build

Find Us On Pinterest

your Pinterest presence. That means you are going to have to do some work. In addition, keep in mind that there is much more that you can do. This isn't one of those do this and that is it. No, this is something that you need to do and then maintain. The good news is that setting it all up properly is the difficult part. Once you have that done all you need to do is maintain it.

Pinterest is only one social media network and to really build your business you should have a presence on several networks. Therefore, at some point, you will have to manage several social media accounts. When you reach that stage, look into some tools for syndicating and cross-posting to your networks so that when you post in one location it will be automatically shared to all of the others. At any rate, Pinterest will definitely help you bring your business to a whole new level.

You may be questioning why there are only five steps in this book. And you're right. There are many more steps to ensuring that you build and maintain a successful business presence on Pinterest. It is a process that has an infinite amount of steps. There will always be something for you to post, change, like, share, et cetera. The five steps you will learn will help you build your foundation. Then it is up to you to continue the walls and maintain the house. Think about it, if I wrote this book with 50 steps then it would be overwhelming and no one would read it. Five is a good number that you can easily accomplish in a relatively short period of time. Not only that, but these five steps are very effective and will help you accomplish more than you realize.

Introduction

Therefore, continue reading and make sure to pace yourself. You can either read this book straight through and then go back to each step while you work on incorporating it into your business, or you can read the book step-by-step and incorporate them into your business as you are reading. The choice is yours.

The main thing is that you do both. You must read and incorporate. You need to put these steps into action because if all you do is read this book then your Pinterest account is not going to improve. This is important you must put this knowledge into effect and use it to help you build your business. The majority of people who read this will not follow through and then wonder why nothing works for them. Be different - follow through and succeed.

Find Us On Pinterest

Chapter 1:

Why Market On Pinterest

Pinterest is a popular social bookmarking site where people collect photos of their favorite things. They store these photos in places called "boards". A board is simply a file folder that people use to categorize all of their pins. People can follow a user's specific board or they can follow their profile. If you follow someone's profile then you will automatically follow all of his or her boards. If there are some boards that you don't like, then you can unfollow them individually even if you followed their entire profile.

Pinterest is a rapidly growing site that has millions of

users that are all potential customers for your business. These users are actively searching for content that piques their interest. They are also sharing content like crazy and telling all their friends to sign up for an account. In fact, Pinterest is currently the fastest site in history to hit ten million unique visitors doing so in January of 2012.

Take a look at this graph and you will see how quickly Pinterest grew from May 2011 to January 2012. Of course, the numbers are higher now, but this is when they hit the record. Pay attention to the light blue bars on the graph. You'll see that during that six-month period the average user spent an hour on Pinterest. That means that when Pinterest went viral people spent one hour browsing for likable content. That's a pretty long time. And if you have more than ten million people spending an hour a day that means there was a really good chance that your content would be seen by lots of people.

Nowadays, people are not spending an hour on Pinterest. However, they are still spending a significant amount of time. Because the amount of users has gone up since then the average time spent has gone down. Either way, Pinterest is still a very valuable marketing outlet that you can use to build your online presence at no cost to you.

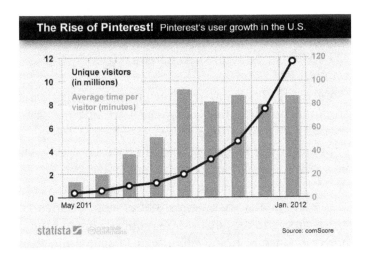

The Rise of Pinterest! Pinterest's user growth in the U.S.

In an effort to grow, even more, Pinterest has created a very helpful feature that businesses can use to keep users engaged. Having millions of consumers was good, but they knew that in order to last they needed to allow businesses to market to their captive audience. They made it possible for account holders to create boards that are specifically aimed at promoting their business. Therefore, you can create a virtual storefront that is completely on Pinterest. This will make it easy for your potential buyers to see all of the products you have to offer in one convenient location.

Pinterest loves it when product sellers do this because it also keeps users on Pinterest for a longer period of time. They have even created a special type of pin called a "rich pin" that product sellers can use to enhance the browsing experience. Rich pins can include additional data to give browsers more information about the pinned product. This is great for you because you can display any important information right within your

Find Us On Pinterest

Pinterest board. It is also great for Pinterest because it helps prevent people from clicking away from their site to find information such as the price.

Pinterest makes it easy for both business sellers and shoppers because they want people to continue using their site. The more people that use their site, the more popular it becomes, and the more their company will be worth. In addition, Pinterest has dedicated lots of time and money to make sure that pins are discovered in search results. That means that unless you spend a lot of time and money on SEO, your products have a better chance of being found in a Pinterest pin than on your own website!

Search engine traffic is extremely powerful because you know that people are looking for whatever they type into the search engine box. Common sense right? If someone searches for something then that is what he or she is looking for. This is obvious now that I said it but you may not have consciously thought about it before. In addition, it is extremely important because if someone is searching for something that is purchasable that means they are most likely going to buy something. If you can make sure your products are displayed in the top of the results then you will significantly increase your chance of a sale.

Thus, the more places you can have your products listed, the better your chances are of turning that web surfer into a future customer. This is basic business presence. The more places you advertise the better chance you have of being found. Using website giants like Pinterest is an excellent way for you to boost your search appearance and be found by more people. Take the time to do a little search on the ranking of your website and then take a look at the ranking of Pinterest. You can use Alexa, Moz, or some other ranking tool.

You'll probably discover that Pinterest is significantly higher than your website and that it ranks right up there with Facebook, Twitter, and Amazon. In addition, if you take a look at the backlinks that link to Pinterest you will discover some amazing results. Pinterest has millions of backlinks and that is one of the reasons Pinterest ranks so high. Several other high-ranking sites are linking to it because they share their content on it to help boost their own site. It is sort of a win-win agreement.

In case you are not familiar with the term, a backlink is simply when one site links to another site. They are extremely important for a website's standing. Basically, the more backlinks a website has, the higher it will rank. The reason for this is because the search engine bots reason that if a site is linking to another site then the other site must be good. Therefore, the bot gives it a boost. The more credible the site that links to it the more of a boost it gets. Thus, if a website has a lot of other credible sites linking to it then the bots believe that site is off the charts. If you would like to read more about website ranking and backlinks take a look at the articles on my blog. However, the bottom line is that the more credible backlinks a site has the higher its rank will be.

Why do you think Amazon is almost always the number

one ranking shopping site? It is because they have so many people signed up to promote their products. There are literally millions of people out there giving Amazon backlinks in the hopes that they will receive an affiliate commission. With that many backlinks, Amazon is sure to rank well.

Pinterest and other social media sites operate the same way. There are so many people sharing content that links back to them that they get a huge boost in search results. In addition, because Pinterest spends so much money to improve their standings your business will have a much better chance of being found there than on its own. Pinterest's budget is no doubt much larger than yours so take advantage of it.

In addition, at the time of this publication, the average Pinterest user spends about 15 minutes on Pinterest each time he or she visits. That number spiked when Pinterest went viral in 2012 and over the past couple of years it has stayed right around 15 minutes. This is a long amount of time for people to be browsing a site. That means your products have a really good chance of being seen by the millions of people that visit each day. Here are some other cool Pinterest facts that should help you realize how much Pinterest is used and why it is so important for you to take advantage of all they have to offer.

Pinterest has hundreds of millions of active users that are pretty evenly split between the United States and other countries. By this, I mean that roughly half of the users come from within the US and half from outside of the US. There are over a billion Pinterest boards and almost 100 billion pins. With all of these numbers, Pinterest is sure to rank well.

However, perhaps the greatest statistic for you, as a business, is that Pinterest is one of the top referring social media sites. That means it consistently sends referral traffic to the linked sites within its pins. Facebook is the top referring social media site and Pinterest is almost always the runner-up. Several branded studies have shown that Pinterest is more effective at driving sales than other social media sites. That means it is higher converting than many other social media sites including Facebook. This is most likely due to the pictures that Pinterest has.

When people click through from a pin they are clicking through because they are genuinely interested. This is a highly targeted advertisement. Especially with rich pins because all of the metadata information such as price, size, description, et cetera is located within the pin. This means that when people click, they almost always make a purchase. This is why Pinterest achieves such high referral standings compared to other social media sites.

When it comes to making sure that your pins convert into sales it is important that you fill out all of the information. This is especially important for business rich pins because the more information people have the higher the conversion rate will be for those who click on it. In fact, pins that include a price receive significantly more likes than those that don't. In addition, the majority of brand engagement on Pinterest is done by users not by the brands themselves. That means that all you need to do is get your information out there.

Your followers will continue to engage and share your content thereby promoting your business for you. They will promote your products and share your pins all for free. This is the greatest thing that any business can hope for. Loyal followers that do all of their marketing for them. They are direct word of mouth referrals. This is huge and can really help the success of a business.

The bottom line is that people love Pinterest. It is a very popular and highly used social media site that gets high referrals and helps convert sales. In addition, it is a very trusted authority since over three-quarters of online consumers trust information and advice they find on Pinterest. If it's on Pinterest it must be true! Take advantage of this consumer base and use this information to help you sell your products to them. They are ready and willing to buy.

When you encounter the statistics that Pinterest has produced then it is pretty easy to reason that it is here to stay. Pinterest took the world by storm and there is a lot of money to be made there. Many people may talk about getting on Pinterest but very few will have the determination to see it through. If you follow the steps in this book you will gain the knowledge and understanding you need to start making an impact in the Pinterest space.

Chapter 2:

The History Of Pinterest

The name Pinterest is a play on words that combines the words "pin" and "interest". Remember the old saying "put a pin in it"? Yeah, Pinterest reasoned that the motivation for putting a pin in something is because he or she was interested in it. Thus, you have the "pin". Although this doesn't really help you with your business, it is interesting to know the rationale behind the Pinterest name. In addition, it is a nice fact for you to break out at your next gathering.

Find Us On Pinterest

As we've discussed, Pinterest is a board style photo-sharing platform that encourages users to like and save their favorite items. They can create theme-based collections for easy categorization. It is a virtual file folder organization system where everything has a place. Users can follow other users or only certain boards. In addition, people can browse all of the pins and create their own boards by adding other people's pins without posting anything themselves. This makes for great publicity and advertising for your business products.

Ben Silbermann, Paul Sciarra, and Evan Sharp founded Pinterest and it is currently funded by a group of entrepreneurs and investors. Below are some of the important events in the Pinterest Timeline. Due to the fact that Pinterest really made an impression in the social media space, I'm not going to list all of the events. Instead, there will only be a list of the highlights. If you would like to learn more about the significant things Pinterest did then you can look up all of the statistics online. I'm sure Wikipedia has a very long list that you can read and take at face value.

The History Of Pinterest

December 2009 – Pinterest begins.

March 2010 – Site launches as a closed beta test.

Ben Silbermann personally wrote to the site's first 5,000 users and offered them his personal phone number if they had any comments. He even met with some of these users to hear their feedback.

Pinterest use grew quickly and climbed to 10,000 within the first year.

August 2011 – Time magazine listed Pinterest as one of the 50 best websites.

September 2011 – Pinterest launched its mobile site.

December 2011 – Pinterest became one of the top 10 largest social media websites.

January 2012 – Pinterest became the fastest site to break 10 million active users.

March 2012 – Pinterest became the third largest social media website.

May 2012 – Pinterest valued at 1.5 billion dollars.

October 2012 – Pinterest launches business accounts.

Second Quarter 2013 – Pinterest hits 50 million users.

June 2015 – Pinterest launched "buyable pins" adding

Find Us On Pinterest

a buy button directly within a rich pin.

October 2016 – Pinterest hit 150 million active users.

June 2017 – Pinterest valued at 12 billion dollars.

You get the idea. Pinterest has rapidly grown from nothing to a major social media player in less than ten years. It reached 10 million users faster than any other company and really skyrocketed. Their business design and platform is like nothing else on the market and they are dedicated to creating an amazing user experience. Any founder that personally contacts 5,000 people looking for their feedback is sure to succeed. Pinterest is a social media giant with a captive audience that is simply waiting to see your products.

If all of these stats have shown you anything it should be that you now know, without a doubt, that you need to be on Pinterest. However, before diving into the steps to effectively build your presence, take a look at the next chapter to learn about some of the most basic things to do on Pinterest. I promise this chapter will be brief. You may already know about these things but it is important to have a basic understanding of how it works before we can move onto the steps you need to take to build a good business presence on Pinterest.

Therefore, take a few minutes to understand the jargon behind Pinterest. Learn how it works and where things are so that you can have a better idea of how to use them when you start marketing. Practice makes perfect and since social media is always changing you are going to always need to practice. Don't worry about making mistakes because when it comes to posting on social media there are no mistakes. There are only things that you can do better. Therefore, learn by doing and always work to make your future posts better than your older posts.

Find Us On Pinterest

Chapter 3:

What Can Be Done On Pinterest?

As you know, Pinterest is an amazing platform where you can do many different things. Since this section is going to be brief we are not going to get into all of the things that you can do on Pinterest. That would be an entire book on its own and still not be enough. Instead, we are going to cover the basics. Hopefully, you are already familiar with this material so this will be a little bit of a review.

If, however, you aren't then I encourage you to do a little bit more experimenting and learning to increase your understanding. Spend a little bit of time

Find Us On Pinterest

on Pinterest examining the layout and how it is all structured. You may also wish to take a look at some YouTube videos about Pinterest to get a feel for how it works. Make sure to find current videos so that you will be looking at the same thing the video is showing.

Pins

The first thing you need to know is that people don't make posts on Pinterest like they do on other social media sites. They make a "Pin". A pin starts with an image or a video and you add it to Pinterest by pinning it. You can add pins from a website by using the Pinterest sharing button or you can paste in a link. In addition, you can also pin media from your computer by uploading it directly to Pinterest. All pins must be media based, meaning they have to have a photo or video in order to be displayed.

Pins can be liked by other Pinterest users, added to their boards, and repinned. It is important to note that even if none of these actions happen on a particular pin that that pin is still going to show up in search results. In addition, it will still have a good chance of being found by random users. If users like your pin, then the standing increases. If they add your pin to their board then the standing is increased even more. If they repin your pin then the standing is really increased.

Therefore, you need to strive to get as many people to do as many of these actions as possible. Then you will really succeed at growing your presence on Pinterest. Of course, it will take several actions by many different users to really increase the standing of a pin. The more actions on a particular pin, the more Pinterest will promote that pin for you. This is a huge bonus.

Boards
Boards are places where people can save pins. They can add their own pins or save other people's pins. Boards are like file folders. People use them to organize their pins by topic or category. It is basically a subpage of your main Pinterest profile. You can name a board anything you want and add a description. In addition, boards can be private or public and you can invite other people to add pins to your boards as well.

People can choose to follow specific boards created by users or they can follow the user to follow all of his or her boards. Creating boards allows you to really hone in on your niche. It is great for targeting specific groups of people and getting them to buy your products. With boards, you have the ability to really find out what interests your followers. Basically, you should have multiple boards on your Pinterest profile and each board should be specific to a particular sub-niche. This way, you will know exactly what interests the followers of a particular board.

Interests
Interests connect everything on Pinterest. Remember the play on words? Pin plus interest equals Pinterest. This is extremely important because it allows you to see exactly what your followers are interested in. If you can find this out then you can tailor and promote specific products to them to increase your chances of making a sale. You can also interact with them

by pinning things that you know will interest them without prodding them to make a purchase. This will go a long way to building up loyalty and trust.

People like to see things that interest them. They don't like to be hounded for a sale because then they start to believe that you are only in it for the money. They need to believe that you are in business to help them. If you are in business to help them then you are going to succeed. However, if you are only in business to make money then you might as well give up now because you are going to fail.

That being said, if you focus on providing for your customers your bottom line will follow. You will make money. Once the customers know you are in business to provide a good product and to satisfy their needs then they will be more than happy to help you by paying for those products. In addition, they will most likely help you promote those products through referrals as well. Therefore, focus on working for your customers, not for money.

Accounts

There are two types of accounts that you can create on Pinterest. Those are personal and business. Of course, you can do many things with both accounts and you can use a personal account for business or a business account personally. However, depending on the type of account, there are certain extra features that may be helpful to you. Therefore, it is best to use both of them. Get a personal account for yourself, if you want, and get a business account for your business. No matter what, get a business account for

your business. The personal account is less important. If you have a business, then you need a business account. Get one!

Personal Account

With a personal account, you can pin links to other websites and share content. You can create boards, add pins to boards, repin other pins, and much more. You can like, pin, and share to your heart's content. You can build up quite a following and get some great engagement. You can even make money with a personal account by promoting affiliate products. However, if you continually promote things with the purpose of making money then you may get banned for improperly using a personal account. Therefore, if you wish to make money on Pinterest, get a business account.

Personal accounts are great for people who wish to browse Pinterest and find trending topics to look at and buy. They are perfect for individuals who like to spend their time surfing the web to look at what's in and what's not in. They are not good for people who want to use Pinterest to make money or increase their online presence. They are not good for people who are highly motivated to succeed. If you are highly motivated to succeed then you need a business account. Therefore, as I said, you need to get a business account. Then, use your personal account to promote your business account.

Help millions of people discover your business and share it with others.

Join as a business

Business Account

A business account is a Pinterest account that is designed to make money. This is the real deal. It is where the rubber meets the road and you will start going somewhere. If you have a business then, duh, you need a business account. It is a level up from a personal account in that there are additional options and features that are very useful for promoting products and services. In addition, you can do all the promotion you like and not have to worry about getting banned. Score.

Pinterest really cares about businesses and wants to help you make money. They have dedicated countless amounts of time, money, and resources toward making sure that you achieve results using Pinterest. The point is that Pinterest quickly realized that they had a captive audience and they wanted to help businesses reach that captive audience. Therefore, they created tools especially for you. Use those tools for your benefit and make your business presence on Pinterest a success. You can take a look at some of the business success stories here. https://business.pinterest.com/en/success-stories

As you can see, Pinterest is a great platform and you can really do a lot with it if you dedicate the time required to learning how to use it effectively. Now that you are aware of what Pinterest is, why you should market on there, and how it began you are ready to start building your presence. Therefore, dig into the following sections because they are exactly what you need to gain followers and convert those followers into customers.

Find Us On Pinterest

Chapter 4:

5 Steps For Creating An Effective Pinterest Presence

There is a lot of work that goes into building a great Pinterest account. It takes extensive thought, detailed analysis, and religious planning. Even though there are more than five steps to being successful on Pinterest, these steps will significantly help your business presence. Therefore, use them and try to incorporate as many of them as possible in your Pinterest business strategy.

I will thoroughly explain each of the five steps and go

over them in detail. However, before that, you should know what they are. This way, if you need one more than the other you can jump to that section. These steps are listed in order so you should accomplish them in that order. If you believe you have already completed one of the steps, take the time to skim through the content to see if there is anything you need to modify on your Pinterest account. Once you finish all five steps, you will be very well set up to rapidly build your Pinterest base. With that, here are the five steps.

Step One – Select Your Niche And Target Market

Step Two – Create The Right Pinterest Account

Step Three – Optimize Your Profile To Get More Traffic

Step Four – Create Your Boards And Start Pinning

Step Five – Promote Your Account To Get More Followers

Step One –

Select Your Niche And Target Market

The first step to creating a great presence on Pinterest is to select your niche. You need to know what you are going to be promoting. Simply put, your niche is your business industry. If you are already in business selling a certain type of product then that is your niche. However, if you are looking for products to promote through affiliate marketing or some other sales method then you need to figure this out.

Choosing a niche is very important when it comes to sales. This is because you need to be able to offer specific products to your customer base. If they see that you have all kinds of unrelated products then they will not be as loyal. The reason is that they may or may not be interested in all of your pins. If you are pinning multiple niches, then your account will be less structured. In addition, it will be more work for you to keep it organized. There is nothing wrong with this but make sure you have lots of boards so you can sort everything out.

On the other hand, if you are consistently pinning products related to a certain niche that interests them, then they will be much more likely to continue to pay attention to your posts. They will become an audience that engages with your pins and continually shares your content. If they can know that everything you post will be related to their interests, then they will be very loyal followers.

Therefore, find a good niche that encompasses a variety of products. If you select a nice wide niche with lots of sub-niches and related items, then you will be able to pin things that do not require a purchase. This means posting niche related content that you will not make any money on. This is purely informational or enjoyment content and it is done for your followers. They will love this and it will help them to believe that you are in business to help them rather than to only make money. We'll talk more about the importance of this later. For now, choose a niche.

Once you have chosen a niche, you need to figure out who your target market is. One important thing to note is that discovering your target market can also help you find a niche. For example, you may have read some statistics that say the vast majority of Pinterest users are women and the majority of the women on Pinterest are mothers. You, therefore, decide to use them as your target audience by choosing the baby stroller niche.

Conversely, you may already be in the baby products business and you choose mothers as your target market. In addition to mothers, you may select women who are in a relationship and also any married woman. You do this because you reason that if they are in a relationship then they may get married and eventually need baby products. And if they are married already they may have children or grandchildren and need baby products.

Basically, the point is that choosing your niche and target market goes hand in hand. You need to think in black and white terms and use stereotypes. Yes, they may be controversial but they work when it comes to sales. You are profiling and generalizing that anyone who is married may need baby products. Although this isn't always the case, it is generally true. It is a stereotype. Therefore, use them to your advantage to market certain products to certain types of people and increase the possibility of sales.

If you are struggling to select a niche and discover your target market, then these questions may help you visualize your ideal customers. They will help you think in their terms and place yourself in the shoes of your audience. In doing that, you will better understand who you are trying to market towards and what you are trying to sell them. The questions are designed for anyone to use to help hone in on the best target market for their business.

Therefore, even if you already have a niche and an audience it will still be beneficial for you to read through these questions. Use them to see how they can help you refine and better understand your audience. After all, the more targeted your audience the better you can communicate with them. And the better you can communicate with them the better chance you have of making a sale.

What kind of people are you trying to reach?
You most likely already know what type of people use, or need, your product or service. However, you may never have thought about it. These are the people you already have in your customer base. They are the people who use your product or service and who continually purchase it. You may or may not know and interact with these people. However, you know of them and you can easily find out what they are in to based on their social media activity.

For example, if these people buy camping products then the type of people you are trying to reach are outdoor people. If you notice that they like plush décor, pillows, and other things then they are upscale indoor people. Use your powers of logic, reasoning, and deduction to see what makes these people tick. You need to find out what types of people are actively spending money in your niche. This will help you know what to promote and when to promote it. Fortunately, Facebook can help you find all of this information using their ads research tools.

What do these people look like?
Are you marketing toward fat people who need your weight loss product? Or are you marketing toward skinny people who need to bulk up? Are they male or female? How old are they? Consider the demographic information of your target market. What does your ideal customer look like? Bring out all of those stereotypes and think about them. In many cases, sales stereotypes hold true so start using them to your advantage.

This will help you determine what types of products they will like. If they are females with blonde hair, blue eyes, and wear pink fitness gear then you will know that they probably aren't going to be in the market for rock climbing gear. They are most likely going to be into water bottles with straws, athletic apparel, and things that make them look good. Thus, posts on climbing probably are not going to interest them. However, if they are people who like fast cars and speedboats then they may like climbing because of the rush it may give them.

Of course, there is always the possibility that such a person will be shopping for someone else. In that case, they may be in the market for your product. However, this will only happen a few times a year when they need to purchase a gift. Therefore, don't rely on it for your general sales marketing campaigns. It is an outlier and should be cast out of your data pool.

Where are these people from?
This is similar to the demographical information

however it is more focused on where they came from and where they are currently living. Consider the heritage of the majority of your customers and start applying some stereotypes. The stereotypes you want to consider are heritage-based stereotypes. Things like: Asian people are shorter, black people are more athletic, white Americans spend more money, et cetera. Remember that when it comes to sales, the stereotypes often times hold true. Therefore, use them to market to these people.

In addition, consider where they are currently living. If they are living on a farm then you will market differently than if they are living in the city. The type of niche you choose will heavily depend on your target audience and vice versa. If your target audience lives in the city then you are probably not going to sell them tools for farming. You are going to sell them things for indoor and patio plants because that is what they can use.

What are they looking for?
Try to determine the end goal of your ideal client. What do they hope to accomplish by purchasing your product? If it is a big fat person that purchases your weight loss product then there is a pretty obvious end goal of losing weight. However, it isn't always this easy. Still, you can very easily make some general determinations by thinking about what your product or service does. You know what the product is. Do you use it? If so, what do you use it for? Chances are that your customers will use it for a similar purpose.

Is it something that your customer needs to survive

or is it a luxury item? This will let you know if it is a necessity or something to make them happy. Is your item an impulse buy that provides instant gratification? Determine what problems your product or service solves. If you can answer this, then you will know exactly what your customer is looking for. They are looking to remove some pain point in life that your product or service will hopefully help them with. If you know what they hope to accomplish then you will be much better able to sell to them by satisfying that desire.

You need to market to their emotions. People don't buy anything simply for the sake of buying it. In addition, most people are not practical when it comes to making purchases. They buy things to make them feel better or to remove some form of pain or problem in their life. Looks like Freud was right, we are all motivated to seek pleasure and avoid pain. Use the pleasure your product provides or the problem it relieves as a marketing tactic to get more sales.

What kind of information do they want to know?
You know the needs of your customers and what they are looking for. Therefore, what kind of additional information would they be interested in? What other information will be helpful to them? This is where you determine some additional ways of pleasing your customers. You are not going to make money on this. It will be solely for the purpose of providing useful information to your customers. This will help you build trust and keep them loyal.

If you can provide them with some other information

that they need then they will be more apt to stick with your product. You will be much better able to keep their business if you are not always trying to sell them something. People like it when they think a seller is in business to help them. If your goal is to provide for and take care of your customers then they will be happy to occasionally support you. They will also be more likely to share your pins with their friends. Even though you may not be making a sale, you will be increasing your brand recognition.

Would they be willing to pay for this information?
Now that you know what information they want, it is time for you to decide if it is worth charging for this information. If it is worth selling, how much would they be willing to pay you? Is it going to be a subscription service or a one time purchase? In addition, how will you deliver this information? Text, email, online login, et cetera. You need to decide if you want to offer this additional information for free as a service to your customers or if it is worth it for you to try and sell it.

Keep in mind that always trying to make a buck usually doesn't work very well. Often times, the most successful businesses are those that put the needs of their customers first. Therefore, if you are constantly hammering them to try and make a sale they probably won't stick around very long. On the other hand, if you are consistently providing them with good information that they can use, then they are going to like you for a long time. Remember, focus on your customers and the money will follow.

How do they want to get the content?

Select Your Niche And Target Market

How are people going to receive your product or service? Are you selling educational material that is available online or are you sending them physical material? Is this content in video, audio, or text? This may seem trivial but it is important because not all people can use any of these formats. Think about people with disabilities or certain learning styles. A blind person will never watch your workout DVD's, however, they may listen to workout tips and ideas. In addition, those who put in a lot of time behind the wheel may not read your books. However, they may listen to your audiobooks or podcasts.

Knowing the answer to this question is a large part of knowing your audience. If you know your target market then you can tailor your delivery specifically to them. Companies like AmazonFresh, Blue Apron, and other food delivery subscription services have this figured out. They know that their target audience doesn't like to go shopping or plan meals. They also know that they have money and like the convenience of home delivery. Another stereotype in action. Therefore, they send the food right to their door and they cater to those desires. Figure out how you can do the same and your business will thrive.

What are you doing for them?
Your product or service must be doing something for these people otherwise they wouldn't be purchasing it. Even if your product that is selling there must be a related product or service that is. Do some research on your competitors and find out what their product is doing for the customers. Then, think about how you can use that solution to market to other people.

People want a product to help them. After all, most people aren't going to buy something that is useless.

If you can find out what problem your product or service solves then you can sell it based on solving the problem. You can go after a completely different market than if you are selling based on the appearance of an item. You need to show people how it works, not tell them how it works. This is where the practicality of your niche comes into play. Are you looking to target the practical solution and results-based buyers or are you going after the buyers who make purchases on a whim? Decide who is going to purchase it and show them what it will do for them.

What are your competitors doing for them?
In order to answer this question, you need to have a niche in mind. Think of a niche and then start to see who your competitors would be. Then take a look at what they are offering to your target market. This is going to require a lot of research and investigation on your part and it is something that will continue even after you are in business. Knowing what your competitors are doing will greatly help your marketing efforts. Learn from them and mirror their campaigns.

Think of all of the money some of your major competitors spend on marketing campaigns. Use their large budget and vast research to your advantage. If they are using one strategy rather than another then it is because it must be working. Therefore, take it into consideration and use it if possible. This will help you to develop better ways to reach more people. It will also help you build a marketing strategy and craft your pins and boards so that they are appealing to these people in spite of what your competitors are doing.

Can you offer something better than your competitors?
After you learn about what your successful competitors are doing, you can do the same thing with a few personal touches. Simply copy their design and make some changes. It shouldn't look like you copied it. However, the format and layout should be the same. You are copying their method of marketing and delivery, not the content itself. Another great thing to do is to find out what your competitors are not offering and see if it is something that you can offer.

Think about your niche and your target market and see if there is anything else that they may want. People who purchased the products are great sources of information and you can find all of their desires and suggestions online. Check out the product reviews and social media pages for these products or services. Chances are there will be a lot of great feedback that you can use to meet the demands of this target market.

Finishing Up
Knowing the answers to these questions will really help you discover your niche and find your target market. Once you understand your buyers you will be able to give them exactly what they need at the perfect price they are willing to pay. In addition, you'll notice that some of those questions also have a great marketing aspect within them. Use them to help you

market to your audience. Take all of these things and start doing them on Pinterest.

That is the great thing about Pinterest is that you can put almost anything on there. As long as you have some form of media then you are good to go. Use that media to show people your product not tell them about your product. Pinterest is more than a social media site. It is a large audience of people that are waiting to be a part of something. They are waiting to try something new, to share something, to buy something, et cetera. They are waiting to become your customer.

Step Two –

Create The Right Pinterest Account

As mentioned before, there are two types of accounts you can create on Pinterest. They are the personal account and the business account. You most likely already have one, or both, of these accounts set up. Since we are mainly focused on the business side of things I'll briefly touch on the personal account and spend more time on the business account. It is a good idea for you to have both types of accounts and use one to promote the other.

Personal Account
This is the account that the majority of Pinterest

users hold. It is the main account and is found on the main website of pinterest.com. Pinterest makes it easy to create an account by having several different options available. You can use your Facebook or Google account or you can use your email address. In addition, I made a great video on how to create a Pinterest account if you would like to watch it.

Even if you have a business, it is a good idea to create a personal account as well. You are a person after all. In addition, you can use your personal account to help promote your business pins. You can add them to boards, like them, repin them, et cetera. This will help build your brand and encourage your personal followers to see it. You can also follow your competitors with your personal account to keep tabs on what they are doing. Be careful when promoting things for sale with your personal account. If you do too much you may run into some trouble on Pinterest.

It is probably best to use the email address option when creating your Pinterest account. Then you can manually connect your other social media accounts at a later point in time. This way you will have full customization when it comes to your connected accounts and your Pinterest username. However, it isn't that big of a deal because you can always edit and change this information from within your profile later on.

Business Account
The business account is definitely the account you want to create if you want to use Pinterest to make money. There are many advanced features and

additional options and it is specifically designed for selling products. With a business account, you can promote your products and even add buy buttons to your pins. This enables people to purchase them directly on Pinterest and be taken right to the sales pages without having to navigate your website.

Business accounts have many additional features that personal accounts don't have. These features are all designed to help you achieve greater results as a business. In addition, your pins will not be flagged or banned for promoting products and using Pinterest to make money. With a business account, making money is encourage and Pinterest wants you to make money. Your pins will also receive a different status since they are pinned as a business product rather than a personal pin.

Pinterest really loves businesses and they have done a lot to help make the platform as business-friendly as possible. They want you on Pinterest and they want to help you succeed in promoting your business. They know that there are a lot of active users on their site and they want to help you connect with those people. They have created a pool of captive people who are all looking for the next thing to buy. And they want you to sell to those people.

Even though they don't make money for this service they provide, they know that by increasing their number of satisfied users that they will be worth more as a company. Remember what we said about working to satisfy the customers rather than to make money? If you work to satisfy your customers then the money will follow. Pinterest is a prime example of that. They are worth millions and they have never charged anyone to create an account.

Business accounts are found on the business subdomain of Pinterest at business.pinterest.com. Click on whatever prompt is there to get you to join or sign up and you will be redirected to the regular Pinterest URL to create your business account. Be sure to take the time and enter in as much of your business information as possible. This will help you out later when it is time to optimize your profile. Once you have filled out all of the requested information you'll need to confirm your email address. After you have confirmed your email address, you are all set and are ready to begin building your Pinterest profile.

Step Three –

Optimize Your Profile To Get More Traffic

Your profile is a very important part of your Pinterest account. This is where you are going to tell everyone, including Pinterest, about your business. Your profile information needs to be as complete as possible. Of course, this goes for any website that your business is on. The more complete your profile the more likely it is that search engines will find your information. In Pinterest, there really isn't much for you to fill out. Therefore, all you need to make sure of is that you have a name, an image, and fill out the description or biography.

Find Us On Pinterest

Editing your profile is very simple. Depending on Pinterest updates, this process may change. Therefore, I'm not going to go into a detailed tutorial on how to edit your profile. Instead, here are some generic instructions that will point you in the right direction. Up in the corner next to your profile picture you should see three dots. When you click on these dots there should be a setting option. Click on that to edit your profile. This may change so if "settings" isn't there look for something called "edit" "profile" "account" et cetera.

Try to write your profile so that it will appeal to your target market. They are the people who will eventually be reading it and making the decision of whether or not to follow you. Therefore, write it so they will like it and want to follow you. Of course, many of them may not read your profile but some will. In addition, if you write it so that it appeals to them and include some popular search terms, then there is a very good chance it will come up in their search results or suggestions.

If possible, use the same name and image across all of your social media profiles. You are building a brand and a major part of brand recognition is consistency. If you are consistent on all of your social media profiles, your customers will easily be able to find out who you are when looking to connect with you on social media. In addition, it will also considerably help you. You will be able to save a lot of time and mental strain by keeping everything uniform.

If you are a business then your image should be your logo and your name should be your business name. If you are an individual then your image should be you and your name should be your name. You could also use a picture of whatever your profile is about. In the same way, your name could be changed to a keyword phrase that relates to your general posting category. Don't get carried away with changing your name all of the time. Generally, it should stay the same so people will always know who you are.

One of the reasons that an individual may not use his or her name would be if you have an account that is all about camping gear. Your account name may be a camping gear keyword and then your boards would be titles using all of the more specific sub-niches. In addition, your profile picture would be something related to the camping gear niche. This is called branding your profile.

Your username should be as close to your account name as possible. This way people will be able to relate the account name and username together. It will help them find it and remember it. In addition, it will also help you if you continually use the same variation across all of your other social media accounts. Generally, it is a good idea to use your business name, your name, or your niche.

When it comes to the description, don't merely copy it from another social media profile. No, write a brand new description. This is important because then the SEO robots will see that it is new content. They will begin to find your social media profiles all over the web and if they all have differently written content then they will think it is original. They will recognize you as an individual instead of a spammy profile that is on every social media site. Then they will begin to boost you in search results and will for sure start suggesting your content. This will really help you get found online and build your brand.

On the other hand, if they see that it is all the same, then they may not suggest your content because they don't want to display multiple pieces of the same information. For example, they won't show your post because they'll think you probably posted the same post on all of your social media accounts. Even though this logic is correct, you still want them to show your posts even if they are all the same. They most likely will be the same because when you post on one social media account you should also share that post with all of your other social media accounts.

It may also be a good idea for you to place some links to your other profiles within the descriptions of your social media profiles. Therefore, take all of the links to your profiles and paste them in each of your other profiles. Some sites, like YouTube and Google Plus, have places where you add these links. However, on other sites, you'll have to paste them in the about section. Doing this will help direct people to your other profiles thereby increasing your followers.

If you make sure your profile is as complete as possible then you will have a much better chance of standing out in the search engines. In addition, you will bring a lot of power to your Pinterest page because the bots will see it as a "real" page rather than a fake profile. Take the time to fill everything out so it is done well.

Optimize Your Profile To Get More Traffic

Not only will it help you impress the bots but it will also make you look much more professional thereby impressing potential followers and customers.

Find Us On Pinterest

Step Four –

Create Your Boards And Start Pinning

Now that your profile is all filled out and optimized, it is time to create your Pinterest moneymaking machines. Boards are going to be your bread and butter. They are very important and will serve to continually draw in new clients for years to come. You are going to fill your boards with pins. These are your individual product listings that people will click on to get more information and hopefully make purchases. Both your boards and your pins need to be well-done and optimized to increase the chances that a random Pinterest browser will become a follower and eventually a customer.

Boards

A Pinterest board is basically a place where you can store collections of pins. They are like individual storefronts or categories of products. For this reason, it is essential that you keep your boards well organized and optimized. This means that, like your profile, your boards must have all of the information filled out. In addition, try to regularly update your boards by adding new pins if possible.

Like everything on Pinterest, creating a board is very easy. Chances are it is the first thing you will see after creating your Pinterest account. There will be a large square with a plus sign and the words "create board" for you to click on. Once you click this, you'll get a popup asking you to name your board. Give it a good, catchy, and keyword-optimized name and click create.

You're not done yet. Even though you filled out all of the information that Pinterest asked for, there is still more to do. Now you will see your board in addition to the square with the plus sign. If you hover over your board you'll see a pencil appear. Click on that pencil to edit your board. If you don't see the pencil then you can click on your board and look for the settings, the pencil, or another way to edit your board.

You'll get a popup with the option to enter all kinds of information. Make sure you fill it out in complete detail. If you don't have all of the details then fill out as much as you can and do the rest later. Be sure to fill out the description and the category. If you want, you can set a cover for your board, which is a great idea because the cover will instantly let people know what your board is about. In addition, you can also add collaborators to your board.

This is a great opportunity for you to you add your personal Pinterest account as a collaborator to all of your boards. In addition, add anyone else who works with your business. Having more collaborators makes life easier, so find some people that can work with you to help you build your Pinterest business presence. Make sure they read this book first so they understand what you are trying to accomplish.

Remember that your Pinterest page is like your website homepage, all of the boards are the individual pages, and the pins are like the posts that make up your pages. In addition, all of the boards and pins will have their own unique URL's making it seem even more like a traditional website. Each board will target a specific sub-niche in your greater website niche and will be filled with pins that relate to that sub-niche. This is one of the reasons why Pinterest ranks so high in the search results.

For example, if your Pinterest account is about camping then each of your boards will hone in on the camping niche. You may have a board about tents, one about knives, one about clothing, one about fire starters, food, et cetera. Each of these specific boards will be filled with pins that relate to those topics. Whether the pins are promoting products you are selling, affiliate products, or general information is up to you. As long as you are promoting related material and everything is easy to find and well organized then you will be good to go.

Try to create several sub-niche boards that all relate to your niche. Don't worry if you don't have pins in them yet. Your goal is to get the boards up there so that you have a place to put your pins once you start pinning. In addition, it is good to give the search bots a little head start before you start pinning. This way they will be able to find your empty boards and then see that you are adding content. This lets them know that you are active thus boosting your rank. Your boards will grow and, as they grow, the number of followers will increase. Therefore, set up at least four boards for now.

If you already have boards set up on your account, then now would be a good time for you to make sure they are all optimized. In addition, make sure that if there are any pins in the boards that they directly relate to the sub-niche. You may have to do a lot of restructuring but it will be worth it. If you take the time now to set things up properly, or re-set them up, then you will be much better off as time goes on.

Due to the fact that Pinterest has organized their entire platform based on the website model, you have a very high chance of showing up in search results. They have coded their design to mimic a website. Every profile, board, and pin has its own unique URL. This was done to help you get found online faster. If you can use their rank to create your own free website that will be found significantly faster with them than on your own then why wouldn't you?

Create Your Boards And Start Pinning

Pinterest wants to help you get noticed but only if you do the things that get you noticed. They have algorithms that automatically promote you as you trigger certain actions. Take the time to make your Pinterest profile exactly how it should be. You need to fill out everything, be organized, and work hard. Then your boards will be found on Pinterest in no time at all.

Pins

Pins are the posts on your Pinterest website. They are the content that people flock to view. They are the part of your account that is going to show up in search results. In essence, pins are the most important part of your Pinterest account. Without them, there would be nothing. Pins are the content after all. This is why it is essential that you have a good foundation set up for these pins.

Further, it is even more essential that your pins are top notch. They need to be amazing because you have laid a great foundation for them. It isn't enough for your pins to be good. They have to be great. They need to be worthy of everything that you recently set up. Well organized, appealing, and directly relating to your niche or sub-niche. After all, you wouldn't put a straw house on an immaculate foundation.

Try to create at least seven pins in each of your boards as soon as you can. Yes, this is a lot of pins to create right away but it is a good number. Seven will make each of your boards look like there is some good content in there. The page will be full and your boards will not look empty or void of content. Having only one, two, or three pins in a board does not convey a good image. It looks like your boards are incomplete. Therefore, shoot for seven as soon as possible. Then work on gradually adding more as time goes on.

Creating a pin is very easy. Often it is simply a matter of navigating to your board and clicking the square with the plus sign exactly like how you created your board. If you don't see that square, then you may have to click the little plus sign in the corner of the page to add a new pin. Pinterest is really promoting their browser add-on so they are making it harder and harder to create a pin directly from their page. Therefore, you may consider getting the Pinterest browser button to make things easier.

Once you make it through that trial and have successfully clicked on whatever button you used to create your pin, you will be prompted to choose whether you are going to upload a pin from your computer or pin something that is already on the web. Chances are that you are going to pin something that is already on the web. This means using a link and allowing Pinterest to retrieve the meta information from the linked source.

Uploading A Pin
If you upload a pin you will be prompted to select media from your computer. Make sure the media is professional looking and high quality so that will inspire people to click on the pin. Add a good title to the pin and then fill out a short description. Make sure to add a URL if you want to direct people to a certain page if they want to click on it. Finally, choose which

board you would like that pin to be in.

Uploading a pin is a great way to control the pictures that correspond with a link. If you want to send someone to your website but don't like the image that Pinterest is pulling then you can add your own image and enter a custom link to go with your upload. The only downfall of this is that the link isn't counted as a social share because it is tied to your upload. It's still good because it will direct people to your site and give you a social backlink but it isn't sharing the content directly from your site to Pinterest.

Pin From A Website
When you pin from a website you will be prompted to enter the URL of whatever site you would like to pin. This can be a page, post, or anything with a link. As long as it is a public URL Pinterest will be able to retrieve all of the metadata. Once you have entered the link, Pinterest will display several images that correspond to that URL. Simply select the one you would like to pin by clicking the red button in the corner of the image.

Now you will be prompted to choose where you would like the pin to go. You'll see a list of your boards next to the image so all you have to do is click one of them. In addition, make sure you enter a little description of the pin. If for some reason you messed up, don't worry, you can edit the pin later to modify the description, change the board, and even the link.

One thing to note is that you should be careful when pinning several pins from one source website. If you are only promoting one thing, especially if it is Amazon, then you may get red flagged. Therefore, try to create pins from several different sources. Use links from your own website that will lead to affiliate products in addition to direct affiliate product links. It is also a good idea to link to informational sites as well. Sure, you won't get any money for this but it will help the validity of your account and may even get you more followers.

No matter which type of account you have, make sure you fill out all of the information within the pin. If you have a personal account then that means adding a short description and a link. If you have a business account then you need to add more details such as the description, price, link, et cetera. The more information you have with your pin the better chances your pin has of being found. Therefore, if you already have multiple pins on your account, then take the time to examine each of them and fill out any missing information.

Tips To Create Highly Effective Pins
The most important thing is to fill out all of the information. I cannot say this enough because so many people wonder why their pins are not being found yet they don't have anything filled out. How can they be found if you don't tell the search engines what your pin is about? The answer is that they can't. Therefore, go through all of your existing pins and get them completed. It will be worth it. I promise.

In addition to that, make sure that your pins are very relevant to your boards. If people are visiting your board on fire starting then they don't want to see pins on sleeping bags. Place those in the sleeping gear board. Now, if you have a funny video of some poor guy catching his sleeping bag on fire then that may be a good addition to both the fire starting board and the sleeping gear board. People will appreciate the change and like the entertainment.

Another thing to remember is that even though Pinterest is a photo-sharing site, you can share videos. In fact, you need to be sharing videos if you want to rank at all. The reason is that so many other people are sharing videos by the millions on Pinterest. You need to keep up with them by sharing your own videos. This is a great way to make sure you are posting from multiple sources and not always promoting products to make money. Make sure your videos are relevant to your board's sub-niche and pin away!

It is important that you use good images when creating your pins. Your images need to be intriguing and inspire people to click on them. For this reason, make sure they are high resolution and that they have some action in them. People like to see excitement and will be more likely to click on an image if it shows that something is happening. Never use clickbait. That means don't use images that people will click on to lead them to something that is unrelated.

For example, most people will click on pictures of cute animals or highly attractive people. If you use those images to promote your camping niche then that is clickbait. However, if you have a cute animal sitting in a tent then that would be okay. The point is, use images that are going to tell people what they are going to see when they click on the image. You need to be honest, upfront, and transparent. This way people will know exactly what they are going to get by following you.

It may also be a good idea for you to spend some time searching for the most popular and trending pins on Pinterest. You can take a look at all of the trending pins by clicking on the "explore" tab and browsing the trending topic. In addition, take a look at the topics related to your niche and see what pins are popular in that category. Take a look at the number of saves, or re-pins, and make a note of what those popular pins are about.

Take the time to search on Google for other websites that are talking about Pinterest. Look for trends, top pins, popular pins, popular boards, and hot topics within your niche. Google will show you tons of great information that you can't get on Pinterest. This is because Google is designed to rank and categorize all of this information. Therefore, use it to your advantage and start pinning things that are already ranking.

Try using Google Adwords to research popular keywords in your niche. Google will tell you exactly how many times people are searching for those keywords and how many hits they are getting. The more hits it gets the more popular it is and the better chance your pins will have at being found. In addition, you can find out how much people are paying to advertise for those keywords. The higher the cost per click, or CPC, the more money people are paying. This means it has a high market value and you may do well to start pinning about it.

You may also wish to take a look at the retail websites that are related to your niche. Check out places like Amazon, eBay, Overstock, Walmart, Best Buy et cetera. Find out what the best selling products are in your niche and see if you can create some pins that promote them. If they are best selling products then the chances of your pin going viral are much better. Not only that, but you can also receive an affiliate commission for referring people to the website.

However, don't merely stop there. Instead of simply posting a link to that best selling product, take it a step further and start looking for good videos that review that product. Pin a few. Then try to find some great blog reviews. Pin them as well. Better yet, get the product and create your own video and blog reviews. Then pin them! This way you can be sure you get credit for making the sale. In any case, pinning best selling products will help you get more followers even if you don't get credit for the affiliate sale. Therefore, do it because it will help build your brand and satisfy your followers.

Finally, it may be a good idea for you to save some other people's pins to your own board. Create an additional board called "Outsiders", or something like that, and save all of the re-pins to it. This will help keep it separated from your boards and also help you get more followers by promoting additional topics. In addition, the creators of those pins may follow you if they see you are re-pinning their content.

Find Us On Pinterest

If you re-pin pins that have a lot of re-pins already then you know that people will continue to re-pin it. Say that five times fast. This will be very helpful to your account because if others re-pin it from you then your popularity will increase. You will also gain many more followers because that viral pin will be seen by lots of people.

All of these tips will help you create better pins that will be more likely to stand out and get noticed. The more you can stand out on Pinterest the more likely you will be to get more followers and eventually more sales. Therefore, take extra care to do all of the things mentioned thus far. The only thing it will take is your time. If you want to succeed, then you need to dedicate the time to do so. Once you have all of the groundwork laid and are starting to create some great pins, you will be able to start promoting them.

Step Five –

Promote Your Account To Get More Followers

Now that you have created some amazing pins to fill your boards, you are ready to start getting some followers. If you already have followers and have finished restructuring all of your boards and pins then you are ready to drastically increase your followers. Keep in mind that you can have the greatest Pinterest page in the world but if you don't have followers then your page is not the greatest.

Pinterest followers are the key to your success because they possess a lot of power. You need to rely on, and take advantage of, this power. The only way people are going to see your pins in their Pinterest feed. This feed is different for every Pinterest user and it changes and populates depending on the interests of that particular user. The pins in his or her feed are automatically sorted with the most recent pin at the top. This is the case for both time of creation and when they followed you. For instance, if they follow one of your boards all of those pins will show at the top of their feed even if you posted them a long time ago.

If they are following your entire account, then they will see all of the pins you post. If they are only following one of your boards, then they will see all of the pins that you make to that board. If they are not following you then the probably won't see your pins. However, they may see your pins if they have shown interest in related topics. The feed is the first thing that people look at when signing into their Pinterest account and it is one of the most seen places on Pinterest. Therefore, make sure your pins are stand out because this is where they need to shine.

Once someone sees your pin on their home feed, they can do several things. They can save it to their board, share it with their social media accounts, share it with a Pinterest friend, comment on your pin, or click the link to go to your website. Of course, they could also do nothing and pass over it but let's not dwell on that possibility. Even though all of these things are great the sad truth is that many users only perform one or two of the actions.

Most people will click on the pin and then click again

to navigate to the site if they are really interested in the pin. Then, many people will save the pin to one of their boards, or re-pin it. Fewer people will share your pin to other social media sites, and even fewer people will comment on your pins. Of course, the amount of interaction you receive on each pin will vary depending on who finds the pin and what they are interested in at the time.

In any case, the most valuable and most helpful thing that someone can do for you is to save your pin to one of his or her boards. Yes, you want them to make a purchase, however, if people start saving your pins then that means all of their followers will start seeing your pins in their Pinterest feeds. This means you are getting tons of free advertising to a network of people that you don't even know. This will really help your business and will serve to get you more followers and, eventually, sales.

Of course, before they start saving your pins you need to get them to follow you. This is much easier said than done and only requires a little bit of time and effort. The first thing you need to do is announce on all of your other social media accounts that you have a Pinterest account. Ask all of the people to follow you on Pinterest and share some of your pins and boards. Chances are that a good number of people will follow you on Pinterest because they are already following you on another social media account.

If you run a business, then you most likely have an email list. It is one of your greatest business assets and you use it as a great line of communication to your customers. How much time and effort have you put into growing that list? It was a lot of work, wasn't it? Fortunately, getting people to follow you on Pinterest is going to be much easier.

The follow function on Pinterest has exactly the same purpose as your email list opt-in form. The purpose is to collect a person's information and create a list. Then, you can market to that list by contacting them when you have something to share with them. The difference is that when you collect emails you are building your own list that you have to manage. When you collect Pinterest follows, Pinterest will manage the list for you. What's even cooler is that the majority of people, especially women, spend more time checking their Pinterest feed than checking their email. (That means you have a much greater chance of reaching them).

In any case, the purpose is the same. You are collecting information to build a list and then marketing your information to that list of people. The difference is that you don't have to do the work of managing that list. In addition, you don't have to pay someone to manage that list either. There are a number of other great differences that I want to point out. Hopefully, you will see that even though you don't have complete control over this list it is much better to focus on building Pinterest followers than traditional email followers.

Pinterest Follows Vs Email Opt-in
Building your Pinterest list need to be a priority for your business. This doesn't mean you should stop

building your email list. Both lists are good for your business and can really help you build your brand. In fact, if you already have an email list then you should send everyone an email promoting your Pinterest account and asking them to follow you. If not, then don't worry. Here are some reasons why a building a Pinterest list is as important or more important than a traditional email list.

Ease Of Use
Opt-in forms are an annoyance for most people. They pop up on the screen and block the content. Many people don't like giving out their name let alone their email address. Therefore, many opt-in forms now only ask for an email. Even still, this is very difficult to get. Not to mention all of the time and effort that it takes to integrate your opt-in form with your website and autoresponder. It also takes money to keep it all up and running.

A Pinterest follow, on the other hand, is very simple. All people need to do is click the follow button and they're done. It is all automatically set up for you. You don't have to do anything. There are no bothersome pop-ups, there is no configuration, no changing any settings, no worrying whether or not it will be compatible with your theme, plugins et cetera. Not to mention, it is 100% free!

Known Intention
When people opt in to your email list there isn't really a way to tell exactly why they opted in. What are they interested in? Hopefully, they are interested in everything you are promoting on your website.

However, if you are promoting multiple different niches then knowing exactly what they want can be difficult. Unless you have multiple lists, which can be a lot to manage, then there really isn't a good way to target their specific interest even if you do know what it is.

With a Pinterest follow, however, you know exactly what they are interested in. If they follow your board on tents and not your board on backpacks then you know they like tents. It is plain and simple and as long as you have properly set up your boards then you are good to go. Pinterest manages all of the lists and keeps everything separated. You never have to worry about sending out the wrong content because as long as you put it in the right board then it will be sent out.

Real People
Email subscribers can be fake, which can be very problematic for your emailing service. If you have a limit, then sending out a dead email is a waste of valuable resources. In addition to people entering in fake emails, you can also get hammered by bots that are trolling the web looking to use your opt-in form as an entry point into your website. Not only can these bots enter in fake email addresses, they can also try to hack your site, which could cause major problems.

With Pinterest, you don't have to worry about security. The people who follow your boards are real people. Sure, there may be some bot accounts out there that follow your boards but they don't pose any threat. You don't have to pay more if you get more followers. There is no limit! In addition, Pinterest has a team of people and bots looking for fake accounts and they are disabling them each and every day.

Instant Visibility

When people check their email, they often simply glance through the subject lines or see whether or not they recognize the sender. In addition, they may filter out messages based on automatic rules that prevent your email from ever being seen. This means that the people on your list might not be getting your emails!

When people go to Pinterest they instantly see your post on their feed. Not only can they see the sender and the subject, they can also see the content! It is like the email is already opened and in front of them. Then, if they like it, they can easily click it to perform a number of promotional actions, all of which will help you build your brand.

100% Open Rates

When you send out emails, the numbers on your list don't mean anything. You could be sending emails to 1000 people and only 50 of them take the time to open your message. Even more discouraging is that only half of them may read your message. Of course, the more targeted your list the better your open rates will be. In addition, the better your subject line the more opens you will get. There are a number of things you can do to increase your open rates and I encourage you to look into them because making sure people open your emails is very important. If they don't open them, then you might as well not send them.

With Pinterest, you don't have to worry about whether

or not they open your pin because it is already open and displaying right in front of them. You have 100% certainty that they will see your pin. As long as it is showing up on their feed then they will see it. Whether or not they take action will depend on their level of interest at the time. You can attract viewers with your sender name, the title, and a great image.

High Sharing Potential

Okay, so let's say you sent out your email and it was opened. Yay! You made it through the filters and past the subject line test. Now they read your email and like it. Chances are that they will continue to go about their day. Maybe they will take action on that email. However, you can be pretty sure that they are not going to share your email on social media. In addition, it is very unlikely that they will forward it to ALL of the people in their contacts. You may get one or two forwards but never ALL.

With Pinterest, if someone really likes your pin they can share it on their other social media accounts thereby sending it to hundreds of people. In addition, they can save the pin, which will forward your pin to ALL of their Pinterest contacts. They can easily perform these actions with the click of a button. No selecting people, typing a message, or anything else. Simply a click and your pin is instantly shared to a vast audience.

100% Free

Email autoresponders can cost a lot of money. You may pay monthly for a certain number of contacts or you may have purchased a program. In addition, you may have to pay for SMTP or hosting. Not only that, but you need an opt-in form and several of those cost money. As your list grows, you may need to upgrade to a higher package, which will cost more money. On Pinterest, you can have as many followers as you can get. Hundreds, thousands, millions, it doesn't matter they are all free.

Of course, there are many more reasons that you need to focus on getting Pinterest followers but this should really help you see the advantages. If you are using email marketing then you should continue to do so. If you are not using email marketing then you may want to consider starting. Even though it is a lot of work it is still a vital part of any business. Pinterest is much easier to use so you definitely need to be growing your followers. Whether or not you wish to use email marketing will depend on you.

Now that you understand how vital it is that you start accumulating mass amounts of Pinterest followers, you need to know how to do that. There are many ways to grow your followers. In fact, by performing the actions we have already discussed you are sure to start increasing your following little by little. However, you need to increase it by a lot. Therefore, here are a few more things that you can do to really help boost your numbers.

Follow Others
Although this may seem a little off, it is very important. Now that you are starting to make a presence for yourself on Pinterest you need to begin following other people. There is no limit to how many people

you can follow so follow as many people as you like. The odds are very good that many of them will follow you back. This will help boost your numbers and if they start sharing your content then it will really boost your numbers.

Now this part might seem a little crazy, but it is really going to help you out. In addition to following other people, you should start following your competitors. What! Yes. If you start following people who are posting some great content that is related to your niche then you are working your way in to marketing to their list. Ding! Yes, this can be a great way to find some targeted followers that you know will be interested in what you have to offer. If your competitors are significantly larger than you then there is a better chance they will re-pin your content because they won't consider you a threat to their business.

Start following other people who are posting in the same niche as you. You're not really competing with them because there is plenty of space to go around. In essence, you are working together to share great content. If you strive to post excellent content regularly then they may re-pin some of your content to their followers. Now you have reached an additional targeted market that you wouldn't have been able to reach on your own. Many of those people will see your content and some of them will start following you.

You may even consider reaching out to the people who post similar content and strike up a deal where you each agree to re-pin one post a week. Of course, you can formulate any deal you like but the point is to re-pin each other's pins. This will help both of you build your followers. We'll talk more about this later because it is a huge way for you to increase your Pinterest presence.

Drop Some Comments
Commenting is another great way for you to start being noticed on Pinterest. Find some trending pins that have a lot of activity and start weighing in on the discussion. Comment solely for the purpose of commenting. Your goal is to get people to see your name and that is it. Avoid doing any form of promotion or placing links. If you want to place a link in your signature that is fine. However, don't comment with the purpose of promoting something.

When you drop some good informational comments that are meaningful to the discussion or the pin, then people will notice. Many of them may reply and several people will be prompted to click on your name and check out your profile. They will see all of your completed information and your highly organized boards and will probably follow you. Then they may start commenting on your pins and re-pinning them to their followers.

Contacting Others
Another great thing that you can do to get some more followers is to contact people. There are tons of people on Pinterest that are interested in whatever it is you are promoting. The trouble is that those people don't know you exist. Therefore, you have to tell them. If you can let them know you exist, then they will be happy to find you. In addition, they will most likely

follow you and will hopefully become a customer. The trouble is how can you tell those people you exist?

The first way is by following other boards that are related to your boards and hope that the creator of that board will follow you back and re-pin your content to his or her followers. However, since this is heavily dependent upon another person's actions it is only an okay method. A better way is to contact all of that person's followers directly and tell them about your Pinterest page. Since that person is pinning content that is related to your niche, all of his or her followers will most likely be interested in your content. They are a perfected targeted audience that is waiting to see your products.

Doing this will take some time and it isn't exactly easy. It will be a long process of contacting people one by one telling them about your boards. However, it does get results and is therefore worth the effort. Navigate to a popular board in your niche and take a look at the activity on that board. You'll notice that Pinterest will tell you the names of the accounts for the people who have commented on it. You can also navigate to individual pins and see who has commented and re-pinned it.

Once you see all of these names all you have to do is click on one of them. Now you will be taken to his or her Pinterest profile where you can see all of their boards. Look up in the address bar and copy the name that is associated with the account. This is very important. You must use the name that is up in the URL not the name that is displayed on their page. The reason is that the name on the page can be changed. However, the name in the URL is a user ID and is directly associated with their account.

After you have the name copied, go to your Pinterest account and click on the board you wish to promote. You have to promote a board you can't simply promote your account in general. When you are looking at your board, there will be three dots. Click on them and then click to share this board with the user ID that you copied. Paste in the user ID in the field and you will see the picture of the person whose profile you copied the name from. Click on the picture to send them a message about your board.

This may seem like a lot of steps but it is a pretty simple process. You can watch a video on how to do it here. https://www.youtube.com/watch?v=dSfo2P_QNKo

When contacting these people, be sure to introduce yourself and tell them why you are contacting them. Explain that you are letting them know about your board and that you think they may be interested. Thank them and move on. Keep it short and sweet. They need to like that you contacted them, not feel inconvenienced. Then, hopefully, they will begin to follow your board as well as your profile.

If you send out ten or fifteen messages every day then you will soon have tons of followers on your boards. The trouble is that these people will only be following the board that you shared and not your whole account. Of course, you could suggest that they follow your profile as well as the board. Some of the people may even navigate your profile and follow your entire account or some other boards. However, most of them are probably only going to follow the board you share.

Therefore, make sure you share a board to which you post often. That way they will see your pins in their feed. In addition, it would also be a good idea to share several of your boards. Really hone in and share specific boards to specific groups of people. Then, once those people follow your boards, you can share other boards with them. Sometimes they may reply to your message. If that is the case then you can reply informing them of your other great boards. This will help you get a lot more followers in a very short amount of time.

It is going to be a long process but if you stick with it you will rapidly gain followers. This is perhaps one of the most effective ways to increase your following because you can be certain that the people you contact are interested in your boards. If you aren't getting a good reaction from your messages then consider changing what you say in the message. Try sharing different boards. Mix things up and do some split testing. Eventually, you will know what works best when contacting other users.

Partnering
Partnering with other people is also a great way for you to generate more followers. These people should be others that are posting in a related niche. They can be people you contact to set up an agreement, competitors, or simply niche enthusiasts. Whatever

the case, partnering with other people to form a group, or community, board is a great idea because it allows you to share the workload with someone else.

There are several ways to get involved with community boards. You can try to contact people that manage certain boards that are within your niche and ask them if you can be a part of the community. Show them some of the boards you have and direct them to look at your account. In addition, be sure to explain why you want to be added to the community. This may work, however many people assume that you only want to join the community for self-promotion. Thus, your acceptance rate will probably be low.

The best way is to find out who manages the boards and follow that person. In addition, follow anyone and everyone who is posting pins in the community board and then wait a week or so. Make sure that your own boards are populated with several pins and that you have a good amount of followers yourself. This will help establish your credibility when the people you followed decide to take a look at your profile.

If after one week they have not followed you back, then you should contact them informing them of one of your boards. Send them a nice introductory message and ask them to follow you. Hopefully, they will follow your board and start seeing some of your pins. Wait another week or two and once you know they have had the chance to see your pins you can ask to join the community. Now they will be able to get to know you before you give them your request.

Find Us On Pinterest

Basically, before asking to join any community boards you need to make sure you have five, or so, boards with at least ten pins in each. In addition, it would be good if you had at least 50 followers. Then, follow the people who are managing the community board. Wait for them to follow you back. If they haven't you back after one week then contact them sharing one of your boards. If they haven't followed you after two more weeks then you may want to move on. If they have followed you, then you can ask to join their community board.

Another option you have is to make one of your boards a community board. You can do this at any time. However, if you are looking to use the community board to grow your Pinterest followers then you should wait until your account is more established. The reason is that several of the high-level Pinterest people will only accept your invite if your board already has popularity. They only want to join you if they see an advantage for themselves. In addition, be careful who you invite because if they start posting spam then your board may get red flagged and reviewed by Pinterest.

Making your board a community board is very easy. Go to your board and click on the "edit board" option. When you see the details, the same place you filled out your description, you'll notice there is a blank space that says, "who can pin". You can add the name of anyone who you would like to allow to add pins to your board. The first person you should add is your personal account or anyone that works with you. This way, when you add higher-level users they will see that there are already some collaborators in the board.

If you are looking for more people to invite to your board, try conducting a Google search that is specific to your board sub-niche. Often times you will be able to find posts from people who are looking for boards with certain topics. Sift through all of the social media posts that Google retrieves and then invite anyone who you think would be a good fit. You may want to contact them first so that they have an idea of why they are being invited. In addition, be sure to review his or her profile so that you know they will be a valuable asset to your board.

Chapter 5:

Conclusion

Hopefully, now you are ready to take your Pinterest presence to the next level. You now understand what Pinterest is and how to properly set up your account so that both people and search engines will find it. In addition, you know how to create well-organized boards and excellent pins for those boards. Therefore, start putting that knowledge into action. Not only that, but you have learned how to grow your Pinterest account by networking with other people. This is important because in order to grow your account you are going to have to connect with, and help, others.

If you work hard to put these ideas into practice and then continue to use them day after day, week after week, year after year, and so on, then your Pinterest account will continue to grow. No, it isn't going to be easy but it will be effective. The diligent prosper and if you continue to be diligent with your Pinterest account then it will prosper.

Thank you very much for taking the time to read this book. I hope it has helped you and that you can use it to grow your Pinterest account and achieve your goals. I'd love to hear from you so be sure to connect with me on any social media site you like.

Appendix:

Resources

Create Pinterest Acount
https://www.youtube.com/watch?v=nYbe0m2Wm-g

Contact Anyone On Pinterest
https://www.youtube.com/watch?v=dSf02P_QNK0

Sell My eBooks and Get 100%
https://spencercoffman.com/become-an-affiliate

About The Author

Spencer Coffman understands the impact that social media can have on your business. That's why he manages and maintains over 40 different social media accounts! He knows what it takes to grow a following and how to convert those followers into customers. Now he's sharing that information with you. So grab your copy today! To read more about Spencer, visit his website spencercoffman.com

Find Us On Pinterest

About The Author

Find Us On Pinterest